THIRD EYE AWAKENING MASTERY

7 Techniques to Open the Third Eye Chakra, Activate and Decalcify Your Pineal Gland

Kate O' Russell

© **Copyright** 2018 by **Kate O' Russell**- All rights reserved.

The following eBook is reproduced below with the goal of providing information that is as accurate and as reliable as possible. Regardless, purchasing this eBook can be seen as consent to the fact that both the publisher and the author of this book are in no way experts on the topics discussed within, and that any recommendations or suggestions made herein are for entertainment purposes only. Professionals should be consulted as needed before undertaking any of the action endorsed herein.

This declaration is deemed fair and valid by both the American Bar Association and the Committee of Publishers Association and is legally binding throughout the United States.

Furthermore, the transmission, duplication or reproduction of any of the following work, including precise information, will be considered an illegal act, irrespective whether it is done electronically or in print. The legality extends to creating a secondary or tertiary copy of the work or a recorded copy and is only allowed with an express written consent of the Publisher. All additional rights are reserved.

The information in the following pages is broadly considered to be a truthful and accurate account of facts, and as such any inattention, use or misuse of the information in question by the reader will render any resulting actions solely under their purview. There are no scenarios in which the publisher or the original author of this work can be in any fashion deemed liable for any hardship or damages that may befall them after undertaking information described herein.

Additionally, the information found on the following pages is intended for informational purposes only and should thus be considered, universal. As befitting its nature, the information presented is without assurance regarding its continued validity or interim quality. Trademarks that mentioned are done without written consent and can in no way be considered an endorsement from the trademark holder.

TABLE OF CONTENTS

INTRODUCTION 1

CHAPTER 1: *What Is the Third Eye?* 2

CHAPTER 2: *Calcification of the Pineal Gland* 7

CHAPTER 3: *Stopping the Calcification Process* 12

CHAPTER 4: *Reversing Pineal Calcification* 17

CHAPTER 5: *Exercises for Awakening Your Inner Spirit* 22

CHAPTER 6: *Understanding Your Body's Energy Flow* 27

CHAPTER 7: *Realigning Your Energy* 32

CHAPTER 8: *Creating Positive Thoughts* 38

CHAPTER 9: *Listening to Your Inner Self* 44

CHAPTER 10: *Shape Your Life with Third Eye Guidance* 49

CHAPTER 11: *Meditation* 53

CHAPTER 12: *Imagery and Visualization* 58

CHAPTER 13: *5-Minute Guided Meditation* 63

CHAPTER 14: *30-Minute Guided Meditation* 65

Conclusion 68

INTRODUCTION

Congratulations on downloading your personal copy of *Third Eye Awakening Mastery: 7 Techniques to Open the Third Eye Chakra, Activate and Decalcify Your Pineal Gland.* Thank you for doing so.

The following chapters will discuss some of the ways your pineal gland, or the third eye in more spiritual circles, can become weak. When the third eye is hindered from working properly, a number of symptoms develop. These can be physical, emotional and spiritual in nature.

You will discover how important it is to maintain the integrity of your third eye and how regular preventative maintenance through proper diet, exercise and spiritual development can help improve the power of your third eye.

The final chapters include guided meditation sessions that you can use whenever, wherever, to begin opening up to your inner self and utilizing your third eye.

There are plenty of books on this subject on the market, thanks again for choosing this one! Every effort was made to ensure it is full of as much useful information as possible. Please enjoy!

CHAPTER 1:
What Is the Third Eye?

The third eye is perhaps the most mysterious, powerful organ in the body. At about the size of a walnut, this tiny organ located in the brain has eluded mystics and scientists alike for centuries. In this chapter, we will discuss the myths and perceived powers of this amazing gland, and what has emerged in the scientific community that supports these ideas.

First, let's go back centuries ago. Thousands of years ago, the exact year doesn't matter, people across the globe searched for answers to their most burning question: What are we on this earth for?

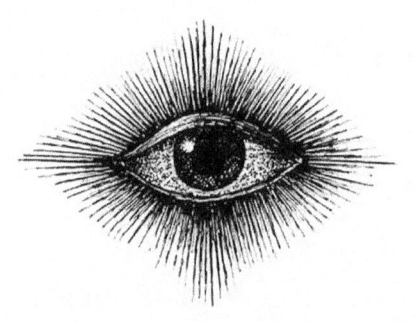

People sought far and wide, experimenting with different lifestyles and means to connect with a higher power, only to come up short. What they found is that all of the answers to their questions, as individual as they were, lay right inside their own mind. The key to life was reaching deep within themselves to find the answers they sought.

The thought across many cultures, most isolated from one another, is that our third eye is the window to our inner selves, our soul, and our connection with the energy and power of the universe.

Creating a deeper understanding of this small area, located on the forehead, just between the eyes seems to be like opening a door into another world. Truly, it is.

The idea that each of us has a soul or an inner self is certainly nothing new either. Our outer self is our worldly skin, what we present in a physical way to others and to the world. We can tangibly see the outer self of everyone around us, and it doesn't change too much. Think of your inner self as a ball of energy, bright and ever-changing that is driving our body forward.

It is this energy that connects us with the energy of the universe. Consider yourself just a small bit of energy in a much larger matrix of energy that creates our known universe. All of the energy is connected, and should you choose to be wholly part of it, you can benefit from its positivity and force. Being in a good flow of energy manifests itself as leading a life that is fulfilling and purposeful.

Let's look at the third eye from a more scientific perspective. The third eye is actually called the pineal gland, a small organ located at the very top of the spine as it enters the brain. It is distinctly in the center of the brain, between the left and right hemispheres. From the outside, it would be dead center between, and just above the eyes. An air of excitement and mystery surrounded this organ as soon as it was discovered. This tiny thing must be important. Otherwise, it wouldn't be tucked away so safely within the brain. What could it be?

The pineal gland is primarily responsible for the production of melatonin, a hormone that is required for regulating our circadian rhythm. It is this vigilance of light and dark that allows us to fall asleep and wake up in a normal pattern. Disruptions in melatonin cause sleep disruption, insomnia, narcolepsy and general fatigue. We will discuss dysfunction within the pineal gland a bit more in the next chapter.

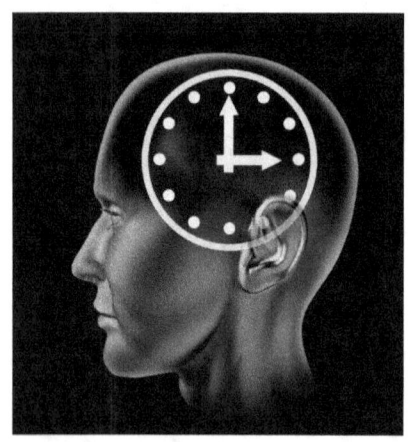

Another curious thing about the pineal gland is that it creates and houses a chemical that is known to cause so-called hallucinations. Dimethyltryptamine (DMT), is naturally produced in the body and can be compared to psychedelic drugs like acid, a man-made version. DMT in large amounts causes the mind to slip into a trance-like state, and vivid imagery occurs. This chemical is released in small doses when we sleep, creating dreams.

For those who partake in the use of psychedelic drugs often report being reborn, awakened into a new life by the experience. This type of drug has been used for centuries in Native American and South American cultures (along with many more) for spiritual practice and connection with the gods. It is hard to ignore the fact that entering such a state opens the mind and has the potential to connect our inner selves with a higher energy. Could this be the key to knowing our inner selves?

Even though the pineal gland is located smack dab in the center of the brain, our inner selves, and our brains don't always communicate with each other. The brain is a strong organ which is driven by organic, analytical thought. Its job is to take in information from our environment, process it, and understand it. The brain is the computer that recognizes what color something is but does not necessarily put deeper thought into it.

Although that example is oversimplified a bit, it is our inner selves that really attach meaning and understanding to things. When the brain and soul are not aligned with each other, it can cause our brain to react without guidance and wisdom of the bigger picture. So, we are required to get in touch with our inner self more often to lead a life with infinite wisdom and guidance.

Awakening our third eye without the help of medications is certainly possible as well. There are many practices we can do on a regular basis that help open the mind and deepen the connection between our inner selves and our analytical brains. The world we live in constantly forces us to work against the better judgment of our inner selves, and so the number of people being spiritually guided are the minority.

What most people don't realize, however, is that they are living in a fallacy of a world in which their physical bodies and analytical minds are at one. The mind and body are disposable, and what is left after we are gone is our inner selves, our spirit, to become connected,  once again, with the energy of the universe. We must do the best we can to live out tangible lives through the needs and desires of our spirit, and not let the worldly needs of the body take hold. Our souls do not need money or power, they need love and understanding. Our time here on earth could be made so much happier and healthier by following the guidance of our inner spirit. Getting connected with our third eye is the key to all of it.

CHAPTER 2:
Calcification of the Pineal Gland

If you feel you are having trouble connecting with your inner spirit, you are certainly not alone. Unfortunately, most of the people on this planet are disconnected and living their lives without guidance from their inner selves. The result is living a life that is somewhat pointless, as there is no drive or desire, or even an idea of what we want. This is not a life worth living.

If you have any of the following afflictions, it may be that your pineal gland, the third eye as it were, is hindered. Take a look to see if you may identify with any of these things.

- Having a hard time making even the smallest decisions.
- No desire or passion for setting or reaching goals in life.

- Find no true joy or pleasure in your daily activities
- Trouble falling asleep
- Trouble staying asleep
- Fatigue upon waking and throughout the day
- No sexual desire or sexual dysfunction

You may notice that many of the symptoms here coincide

with a diagnosis of depression, and that shouldn't be of any surprise. When the pineal gland is not making melatonin, and your sleep schedule is out of whack, the production of happy hormones, like serotonin, does not occur. The result is a tired, sluggish mind, incapable of anything but the bare minimum. If getting through the day is your only goal, you may have a blocked pineal gland. This isn't normal, so don't settle for good enough. This is your moment to find out what is wrong with your pineal gland, so that you may take action to live your best life.

Both the scientific and spiritual communities recognize the calcification of the pineal gland, or third eye, as a major cause of dysfunction in many aspects of life. The idea is that the gland becomes obstructed in some way that disrupts the flow of energy, and the production of hormones. Each recognizes the same culprits as the cause of this disruption.

Calcification is the process of mineral buildup. This can occur anywhere in the body as a result of too much of any mineral in the environment. This may manifest itself as kidney or gallstones, and this residue can build up around any tissue, including the pineal gland. These minerals disrupt the flow of energy and nutrients from the blood entering the gland. Think of it as a hard crust forming over the top of the gland.

Two of the biggest causes of pineal calcification are chlorine and fluoride. Chlorine is the chemical used to kill bacteria in pools and fluoride is added to water to prevent dental caries in the general population. While small amounts of these chemicals are actually necessary for the body in trace amounts, it is very easy to get overloaded with them.

The word calcification implies that calcium itself is a cause, and that is correct. Calcium is one of the most abundant minerals in our bodies, making up the structure of bone, creating muscle contraction and facilitating numerous reactions within the body. We need calcium, and many people are actually deficient. Taking a calcium supplement is very common, but if not taken correctly, could cause calcification of the pineal gland.

Calcium requires Vitamin D to be absorbed and utilized by the body. A lack of Vitamin D means that calcium will float around in the blood until it deposits somewhere. The result is calcification of important glands or deposits of calcium wreaking havoc in the kidneys.

Environmental toxins also play a big role in the calcification process. Any time the body comes in contact with a substance that is foreign to it, there is a question as to what happens to it. The body knows how to process food items and nutrients, but chemicals like pesticides and pollution are somewhat of a question mark. The body can certainly get rid of the bulk of it in urine or sweat, but some chemicals circulate in the blood and build up around the pineal gland.

High levels of mercury and lead end up in hair follicles and other strange places, and toxic levels can shut down organ systems altogether. The fact is, most of us are not exposed to large amounts of toxins like this, but the low-level exposures are still having a major impact on our wellbeing as related to the calcification of our pineal gland.

We must not forget about the things that purposely enter our bodies: food. The choices we make with food every day will affect the function of our pineal gland. When it comes to foreign substances, processed foods take the cake with their use. Preservatives and compounds not normally found in nature are now regularly added to foods to improve texture, quality and shelf life of food products. If consumed in large amounts, the excess has no choice but to settle in areas like the pineal gland.

The unfortunate reality is that our bodies are constantly bombarded with substances that can be harmful not only to the pineal gland but to our organ systems as well. Calcification of the pineal gland will cause a number of issues, starting with the decreased production of melatonin. This will quickly throw off your sleeping pattern causing general fatigue. The result of even a few nights of this can easily derail your motivation and quality of life. You may begin to forget things, be less productive throughout the day.

Over time, these small things add up to a major life issue. As your productivity slips so does that big promotion at work. You feel unmotivated to wake up in the morning, and even less so to explore the wonders of the world. With each day that passes like this, your inner self dims a little. Your brain and spirit become less and less connected, and your purpose and guidance completely disappear. You wander aimlessly, only focused on getting through the next few moments of your life.

True happiness is about looking at the big picture and leading a life full of wonder and purpose, all guided by your inner spirit. Knowing what you know now, how could you possibly go another moment with a calcified pineal gland. If your life could be exponentially better just by making some changes and decalcifying your pineal gland, why wouldn't you? Take some time to harness the information provided in the next chapter to begin the decalcification process.

Once your pineal gland is back up to speed, it will be possible to tap into its boundless potential and reconnect your brain and your spirit. Doing so will leave you with a bigger and a better sense of purpose, and you will live a life driven by infinite wisdom and ethereal guidance. Isn't that the life you want to live?

CHAPTER 3:
Stopping the Calcification Process

The key to stopping the calcification process of the pineal gland hinges on your ability to avoid exposure to toxins that are causing it. While it may not be possible to avoid them totally, we can certainly make an effort to reduce exposure to things that are well within our control. There are a number of things to do daily that will reduce the amount of foreign substances that enter our body.

Let's start with the big one: fluoride. As explained in the last chapter, fluoride is added to public drinking water to reduce dental caries in the general population. Fluoride has been found to strengthen enamel and decrease cavities. Adding fluoride to the drinking water in small amounts has been shown to decrease this incidence.

People with public or city water that is treated with fluoride have the option to use a filter that will eliminate fluoride. Buy a filter that specifically does this, as there may be options that only filter out heavy metals. That being said, a home with well water from a natural spring will not have fluoride added but may have a number of excess heavy metals from the soil in the supply. It is always a good idea to have your water tested to be sure there are safe levels of minerals (and bacteria) in your water. Many types of water filters exist for this as well. Make sure to buy a style that will eliminate the metals that exist in your water.

Fluoride is also found in smaller amounts in products like toothpaste, to prevent tooth decay. Of course, toothpaste is fine to use, but avoid swallowing it to decrease exposure. Pesticide exposure increases fluoride as well. The common fluoride-based pesticide cryolite is used on many fresh fruits and vegetables to prevent bugs. Buying organic fruits and vegetables can certainly limit exposure.

If finances are a concern for buying organic, buy regular versions of foods from the Environmental Working Group's (EWG) Clean Fifteen list. Fruits and veggies with peels that you take off before eating will contain fewer chemicals, as the peel will absorb most. Avoid eating non-organic fruits and veggies like strawberries and celery, where there is no peel. Any pesticide residue will be directly on the skin of the fruit, and therefore, will make it into your body.

A couple other thoughts on fluoride: Green and black tea leaves contain concentrated levels of fluoride. Moderate tea consumption to limit this exposure. The same goes for grapes. Eating excess grapes, raisins or drinking wine can increase your fluoride consumption.

Chlorine is another chemical found to calcify the pineal gland. Like fluoride, it can also be found in public drinking water. It is used as an antibacterial to reduce the risk of foodborne illness from the water. While this is important, the low levels of chlorine consumed on a daily basis build up and cause problems. Drinking filtered water isn't enough. If you are still using unfiltered water for showers, cleaning dishes and brushing your teeth, you are still exposed. A whole-house water filter is the best option to avoid chlorine from the public water supply.

Chlorine is also a major component of household products like laundry detergent. It is the main component of bleach! Consider switching to an all-natural, chlorine free versions of your favorite products. Better yet, make your own to avoid other chemicals foreign to the body as well. Trading out chlorine for something just as toxic doesn't solve the problem, it only changes it.

Another big change to make is to your diet. You have likely heard that eating better, and 'cleaner' is good for your body, for weight loss, and the like. All of those points are true, but even more so when it comes to your pineal gland. These days, foods are being processed at a rate higher than ever before. Food companies regularly add a host of chemicals and compounds to improve the appearance of their product, enhance flavor or prolong shelf life. While these things may improve their bottom line, the effect on our health is astounding.

Chemical fillers that are foreign substances to the body build up around the body. Calcification of the pineal gland is one problem, but these chemicals put additional strain on the kidneys and liver, as they must process them. Compounds that circulate the body often turn into free radicals that damage cells. When cells die more quickly than they are reproduced, the aging process begins. On top of that, damaged cells become physically changed, and can for cancerous cells when they multiply. There really are no positives to these chemical additives, except the immediate satisfaction of enjoying the food.

Long term, we are better off eating things that our bodies are used to. When choosing foods, avoid those that have long ingredients lists, and words you don't recognize. If an ingredient looks like it has a chemical name, it's probably something you don't need. Your body has not evolved fast enough to recognize and process these things. Eat what your body is designed to consume: whole foods found in nature, for the majority of your meals. While you are at it, keep in mind that genetically modified organisms (GMO's) are new to the body as well, and could cause the same issues known chemicals do.

If it is recommended that you take a calcium supplement, be careful of the dose and how you take it. Adding excess calcium will not cause your bones to become stronger if it is 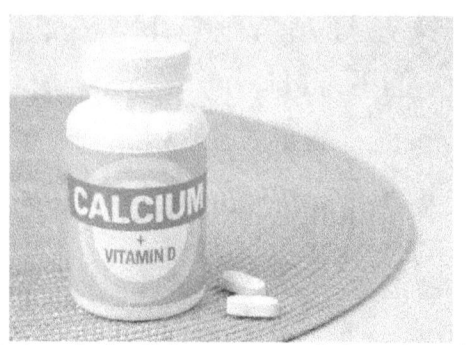 not absorbed. Excess calcium will simply build up around the pineal gland and inside the kidneys. Take the dose recommended by your doctor only, don't overdo it. More isn't necessarily better. In addition, take a supplement that also has Vitamin D to enhance the absorption of calcium.

Going right along with what not to do, we must also discuss stress. Simply saying that you should avoid stress just isn't possible. It is everywhere, and unless you pack up and move into the woods, it is not avoidable. Guess what? The woods have stress too! Learning to manage your stress is the only way to reduce its effect on your pineal gland. You will find that the exercises and practices discussed throughout this book will help reduce stress. Regular meditation, exercise and eating right will all help reduce this stress.

This chapter has basically been a what NOT to do when it comes to pineal calcification. Your awareness and avoidance of things that will continue to calcify your pineal gland is step one in enhancing the power of your third eye. In the next chapter, we will focus more on things you can ADD to speed up the decalcification process and keep your pineal gland healthy. Enjoy!

CHAPTER 4:
Reversing Pineal Calcification

While the last chapter largely focused on what not to do to earn a calcified pineal gland, this chapter will outline the various methods and tricks to reverse the damage already done. Here, we will focus on proper nutrition, essential oils and supplements available that can help speed up the process of decalcifying your pineal gland. Let's begin with a proper diet.

Nutrition: You are what you eat. At some point or another, we have all heard this. In this case, you are a calcified third eye, and it is high time you weren't. In the last chapter, we discussed ridding the diet of processed foods and sticking to whole foods with ingredient names you can pronounce. These are good rules to live by, but what exactly should you be eating?

In general, we should be eating a diet that contains a good amount of protein, from either animal or plant sources. This should make up about a quarter of your plate. Another quarter should be filled with something starchy, carbohydrates for your immediate energy needs. Rice, quinoa, whole grain bread, and fruit falls into this category.

The other half of your plate should be filled with non-starchy vegetables, like salad greens, cucumbers, tomato, and squash.

When it comes to the health of your third eye, organic, non-GMO products are best, as they are generally free from pesticides, residues and heavy metals that can calcify around your pineal gland.

Certain foods enhance the process of decalcification, and adding them to your healthful diet can have you feeling better in no time. Of course, everybody is a little different, so if you are generally sensitive or allergic to any of these foods, steer clear of them. While they may help clear your pineal gland, you may have indigestion or other serious side effects. Always be vigilant of any new ailment when trying a new food.

Foods that support melatonin production will help stimulate a slow pineal gland. Foods with lecithin, a natural emulsifier do just that. Eating beans, eggs (with the yolks), dairy and whole grains all contain lecithin. In addition, dairy products are usually fortified with Vitamin D, which will help offset any excess calcium found in these options.

Foods that provide antioxidant properties are helpful as well. In general, Vitamin C and E are major antioxidants, quickly neutralizing free radicals across the body and sloughing off your calcified pineal gland. Vitamin C is often associated with citrus fruits but is also available in high doses in all vegetables, including potatoes spinach and broccoli.

Higher doses of vitamin C are available in supplements and

may speed the recovery. Be sure to check with your doctor before beginning any supplement. To be a bit more modest, add a tablespoon of lemon juice to your day, either in tea or diluted with water. The acid in lemon juice can be detrimental to your tooth enamel in high concentration, so dilute well or try drinking with a straw, avoid letting the liquid hit your teeth. In fact, other acids, like apple cider vinegar contain malic acid which can help with decalcification as well.

Vitamin E, another antioxidant, is found in nuts and animal products. Using nut oils, like walnut or flax can give you the same benefits of eating an abundance of nuts. Avocado and a number of vegetables also contain Vitamin E. Again, supplements are available as well, but you are better off making some dietary changes rather than filling up on supplements. Surely, your doctor will agree as well.

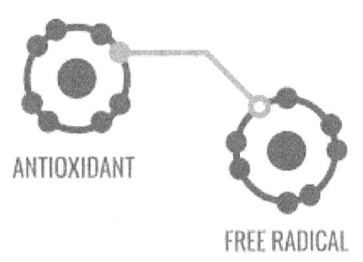

The antioxidant donates an electron to the free radical's unpaired electron.

Another great food item is garlic, which has antibiotic properties, as well as the ability to dissolve calcium. Garlic is great for fighting off infections and boosting your immune system. Unfortunately, to have a decalcifying effect on the pineal gland, it is recommended to eat 1-2 garlic cloves per day. If you love garlic, this is still a bit much, and if you hate it, might sound impossible.

There are garlic capsules available, but if you feel natural is the way to go, try making a super potion out of garlic, lemon juice or apple cider vinegar and walnut oil. This concoction sounds gross, and it is, but you will only need an ounce or two total. It will all be over within one quick swallow, then you can carry on with your day.

Essential oils: Aromatherapy is an ancient method of relieving all that ails the body, including a calcified third eye. It is possible to awaken your third eye with help from essential oils. These oils can also be applied directly to the skin for similar effects. Because they are concentrated doses of herbal remedies, it is important to know how to use them properly to avoid feeling ill or having strange reactions. Keep in mind that using certain essential oils is frowned upon during pregnancy and with certain health conditions, so always check with your doctor to make sure it is safe.

Use cedarwood, frankincense or sandalwood essential oils. Use an oil diffuser to spread the lovely scent through the air. Other options are available too. Apply a drop or two to the roof of your mouth by putting a drop on your thumb and pressing it against the roof of the mouth. You may also take 1 drop under the tongue, or apply 1 drop on the physical third eye on your forehead or 1-2 drops on the crown of the head.

Crystals: There are a number of camps that tout the healing power of crystals when it comes to the third eye. The idea behind using any type of crystal is that when the energy of the crystal comes in contact with the body's energy, it causes a magnetic, 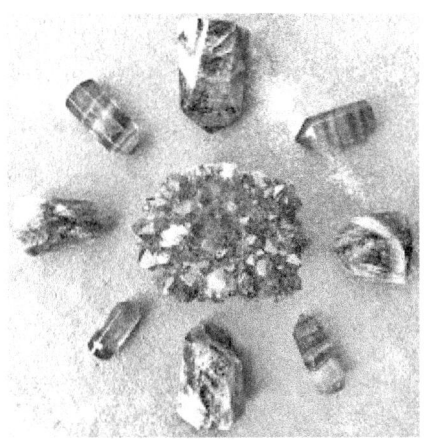 energetic shift, realigning the energy within your body. Indigo and violet crystals are thought to do the most with the third eye specifically. Crystals can be touched to the third eye (center of your forehead) to provide the most benefit. Use Amethyst, Moonstone or Purple Sapphire to get started.

While it is important to do whatever you can to decalcify your pineal gland, stick to things that will fit well into your day. Stress causes quite a bit of calcification on its own, so trying to fit in lots of new things in your day might not be possible. Give each a try and find what feels best to you. If one of these options feels like it isn't doing anything, try something else.

CHAPTER 5:
Exercises for Awakening Your Inner Spirit

Getting your body moving is one of the best ways to clear your pineal gland and get in touch with your inner spirit. We know that when we exercise, our muscles expand and contract, creating physical movement. What you may not realize is that physical exercise also moves energy around the body. The increase in this energy flow helps you connect your mind and body, as well as your mind and inner spirit.

Any type of physical activity will do. Starting a regular routine consisting of cardiovascular activity like walking or running will get the blood pumping and will keep your heart healthy. Adding weight training will improve strength, preserve bone mass and burn more energy. Any type of activity will raise your body temperature, get your energy flowing and will clear a blocked pineal gland.

There are exercises that focus more on the mind and spirit connection, which may fit better into your overall goals. Practicing yoga is a great place to start. This exercise combines the benefits of strength training and stretching with relaxation and meditation.

If you are not familiar with yoga, it is a guided practice in which specific yoga 'poses' are completed. The movement is generally slow, and the poses are meant to work your muscles and stretch your tendons in a way that would not normally be possible in daily life. You may feel muscles and tendons you didn't know existed after your first class.

Practicing yoga should not be an intimidating task. Although you may be surrounded with other people in a formal class, the idea is to only compete with yourself. Your strength and flexibility will improve with practice, and so you are only trying to improve upon yourself, not compare yourself with others. It is not a game or a competition.

There are many different styles of yoga, ranging from a more regimented class, like Bikram, which uses the same set and combination of poses. Bikram is also often done in a hot room, more than one hundred degrees to add a more cardiovascular component to the practice. This will definitely be too intense for a beginner, but for a seasoned yogi, provides increased flexibility and more spiritual connection. The heat requires the mind to focus exclusively on regulating heart rate and maintaining temperature. With the mind preoccupied on that, it becomes a lot easier to enter a meditative state.

If you are practicing on your own, there are a number of poses to include that will help engage your third eye specifically. Any pose that rests your forehead is benefitting the pineal gland. Mountain pose, in which you bend and rest your forehead on your knees is a great one, although it may take a bit of time to increase your flexibility to this level. Staff pose is similar but a little easier from a seated position. Dolphin pose, a modification of downward dog, is another beginner-level pose. Child's pose is perhaps the easiest of all. The forehead and third eye become grounded to the floor.

More classical meditative yoga is also available, in which the focus is more on the breathing process rather than the physical aspect. Either way, you will be  moving your body, increasing energy flow, relaxing and meditating. Yoga is great for helping connect all of your entities, physical, emotional and spiritual. Regular yoga practice will strengthen the body between all three.

Yoga can certainly be a challenge for people who don't move around easily. Although regular practice will improve range of motion, starting with a different type of exercise may be helpful. Practicing Tai Chi is another exercise that has the same meditative properties, but the methods are a bit different.

Tai Chi, although it originated as a form of martial arts, focuses on different poses as well. Instead of being intense and effective for defense, it is a choreographed, graceful movement, constantly flowing from the body. It also focuses on breathing, creating a meditative practice along with the physical exercise. Each pose flows flawlessly into another, with no static pauses, unlike yoga.

Tai Chi is low impact and therefore is open to a greater variety of people. It does not include weight training and does not put a great deal of stress on the cardiovascular system, unlike running or jogging. It is a great practice if you are just beginning an exercise routine. Regular practice has been shown to increase aerobic stamina, increase energy, reduce stress and increased muscle tone.

These benefits are achieved with regular practice, just as with any exercise routine. It is important to maintain a routine to truly feel an improvement in your body and mind. If you are new to Tai Chi, finding a beginners' class is your best bet. Learning the fluidity of the movement takes a bit of practice, but once you get the hang of it, the movement will flow, and you will see more of the meditative benefits.

Regular exercise is mostly about reducing stress when it comes to your third eye. The movement of energy releases tension and increases flow during  times of rest. When you are stressed, your body produces stress hormones like cortisol and adrenaline. The goal of these hormones is to raise your heart rate and stimulate muscles to physically flee from danger. This response dates back to the very existence of humans when there was more incidence of physical peril.

These days, our stress comes from late meetings, work schedules and the like. We are not expending the energy given by those hormones, and it builds up, blocking flow within the energy system. Exercise helps relieve some of that tension so that we may be more relaxed overall.

No matter what exercise you decide on, choose something to do regularly that you enjoy. The true benefits of exercise come when you like what you are doing, and you are not just going through the motions. Switch up your exercise routine to keep it interesting, and don't forget to take rest days when your body is feeling fatigued.

CHAPTER 6:
Understanding Your Body's Energy Flow

We have talked a lot about the flow of energy within the body so far, but what does it all really mean? With the exception of modern western medicine, most cultures have believed in the power of energy since the very beginning. Modern eastern cultures still use this concept as the basis for their health care systems today.

Disruptions in energy cannot be cast aside for chemical-altering drugs and physical surgeries and procedures more common today. To be clear, modern medicine does have its benefits, but it often trumps the basic understanding of energy flow. Many ailments can be treated by balancing energy, rather than providing medications.

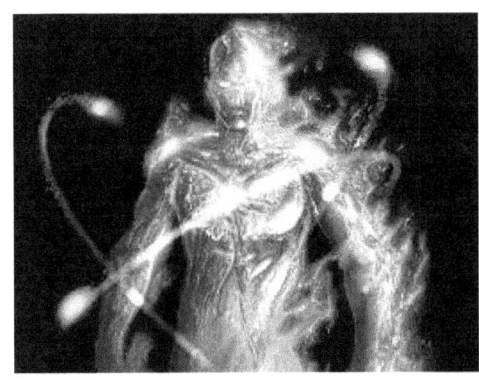

What is this energy flow? We have long known about chakras or energy centers within our body. This idea originated in Chinese culture thousands of years ago. The idea is that there are numerous energy centers within the body, and disruption of energy in any given center can cause physical, emotional and spiritual ailments.

There are seven major chakras, aligning themselves along

the center line of the body. Each chakra is associated with a specific part of the body, mind, and spirit. Decreased or excess energy flow to any will cause a specific reaction. Let's discuss the seven major chakras in detail:

Root chakra: This chakra is located at the base of your spine, at your tailbone. The energy of this center is meant to root you in your daily life. It is what keeps you humble and grounded. It makes you feel safe and secure. When energy is not properly flowing in this area, it causes many things to fall out of place, especially emotionally. You may feel insecure about your living arrangements, struggle with money or feel generally unwelcome in your current circumstances.

On a physical level, you may have issues with a range of motion in your legs, weak knees or sciatica problems. Your immune system is affected by your root chakra. Therefore, you may be more prone to illness.

Sacral chakra: This energy center is located on your abdomen, just below the belly button. It is the center of your greatest desire, sexual function and overall joy and pleasure. If energy is disrupted in this region, it could affect your desire for sex, affecting your relationships. You may also find it difficult to have a passion for hobbies and interests you once had.

Physically, this chakra is responsible for the health of your reproductive system, kidneys, and urinary tract. Energy imbalance may manifest itself with urinary tract infections or infertility.

Solar plexus chakra: This energy center is located near the top of the abdomen, right in the center. It is your core for confidence and belief in yourself. Without good energy in this region, your self-esteem will be virtually non-existent, hindering progress in all areas of your life.

In the physical body, the solar plexus chakra maintains good digestive health and that of the liver, gallbladder, and pancreas. These organs are responsible for digestion and nutrient metabolism, and if they are not at their best, the whole body suffers. An unwell solar plexus may manifest with general gastrointestinal dysfunction, indigestion, diabetes and other diseases of these organs.

Heart chakra: You may have guessed that this chakra is located near your heart. In fact, it's just a little to the right, along the spine, but in line with the heart. As you may have imagined, the energy in this chakra is responsible for matters of the heart, in a physical and emotional sense. It gives you the capacity to love and to feel compassion for others.

It also maintains the physical health of your heart, lungs and total body cardiovascular system. If you are prone to lung infections like bronchitis or pneumonia, have heart irregularities or circulation issues, it may be that your heart chakra is out of alignment.

Throat chakra: The throat chakra is associated with the ability to communicate, both physically and mentally. If you are prone to a sore throat and swollen tonsils, you may be lacking energy in your throat chakra. In addition, this chakra greatly affects your thyroid gland which is located in the throat.

From a mental perspective, this chakra gives you the ability to communicate effectively. We all have days when it feels like no one is listening, or no one can understand the point you are trying to make. This could easily be attributed to a lack of energy in your throat chakra.

Third eye chakra: It should be no surprise that the third eye is an energy center all its own. This energy center is known to be the regulator of spiritual connection. As we have been talking about, a misaligned or calcified third eye chakra will decrease your ability to tap into the wisdom of your inner self. Without this guidance, life becomes aimless and dull. Your spiritual flame will dim, as energy is removed from this energy center.

In a physical sense, a blocked third eye chakra will increase insomnia and fatigue, as your natural sleep patterns will weaken. It may also result in headaches, changes in vision and depression. It is imperative to keep this chakra aligned as these symptoms easily affect the rest of the body, and your life.

Crown chakra: This energy center is located right at the top, or crown, of your head. It is known to be the highest connection between the energy of the universe and your body. Imagine it as the metal rod connecting bumper cars to the energy source above them. It literally brings energy into the entire system.

This chakra is imperative because if it is out of alignment, energy flow will decrease to all of the other chakras. Symptoms include fatigue, a range of physical symptoms caused by low energy in all the chakras, and emotional distress. It is easy to become fatigued, anxious and depressed when you lack the energy to keep your physical and emotional health intact.

Keeping your major energy centers aligned required daily vigilance. As energy is quick-moving and constantly flowing, it is imperative that you are aware of what is going on in your mind and body at all times. Doing so allows you to pinpoint minute symptoms that are associated with a specific chakra. Remember that if one chakra is out of line, it may mean that others are overworked to compensate. If you feel that your life is doing great in one aspect but terrible in others, your entire system is out of balance. Keep an eye on your overall balance every day for your best health and wellness.

CHAPTER 7:
Realigning Your Energy

Knowing where your energy is blocked is the key to fixing it. Energy is constantly moving and changing, and any chakra could be misaligned at any given time. The result is an imbalanced life, and the symptoms of that can be pretty obvious if you look.

Being conscious and vigilant of the subtle cues your body and mind give you is a great way to tell if your chakras are aligned. For example, if you are suddenly developing indigestion with foods that have never given you a problem, your solar plexus chakra may be out of line.

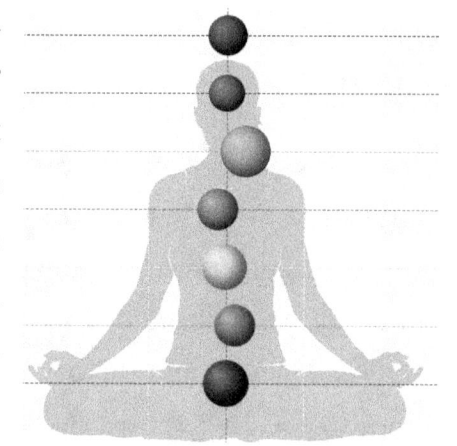

It is important to know how to manipulate the energy of each chakra to realign and bring new energy to the area. Take a look at each individual chakra to find out how to keep it in line. You will notice that exercise in general, along with specifically targeted exercise can help align chakras, as well as a good diet.

Root chakra: Using essential oils myrrh or cedarwood in the methods described in chapter 3 can help draw energy to this chakra. Exercises that root the feet firmly to the ground, like jogging or walking, and yoga poses like warrior can help as well.

Sacral chakra: Use the scent of jasmine to invigorate this chakra. Any exercise that works the abdominal muscles will stimulate energy in this area as well. Try warrior and other yoga poses that draw heat to the body.

Solar plexus chakra: Ginger and lemon tea can really help soothe this chakra. These elements have been recommended for ages to help with general indigestion. Turns out, they have been realigning your solar plexus all along. As with the sacral chakra, abdominal exercises also draw energy to this chakra.

Heart chakra: Practicing conscious self-love and compassion for others is the best way to realign your heart chakra. If you are feeling disconnected from others, make the first move and get involved with people.

Exercises that stretch the chest cavity can help open up your heart chakra. Try cobra in yoga, or simply meet your hands behind your back and open the area. Essential oils like peppermint and thyme help open the respiratory system and are especially helpful if you are dealing with mucus or infection.

Throat chakra: Playing on the idea of opening up air passages, eucalyptus and peppermint oils are great to clear the throat chakra as well. Use honey and lemon to soothe a sore throat, and do exercises that loosen the shoulders and neck. In yoga, do neck rolls or downward dog to release tension in the region.

Third eye chakra: As we touched on earlier, using healing crystals that are indigo can help redirect energy in the third eye. In addition, strong scents like sage help awaken your senses and restore energy to the mind and third eye. Yoga poses that focus on the forehead to the ground, like child's pose, will also be beneficial. Don't forget about meditation as well. More on that later.

Crown chakra: Since this is the chakra that is partially responsible for energy within all of the chakras, it is vital to keep this one healthy. Floral and citrus scents tend to awaken this chakra. It also helps being outside, as you can then take in a greater amount of energy from sunlight. Get in better touch with your inner spirit by being connected with nature.

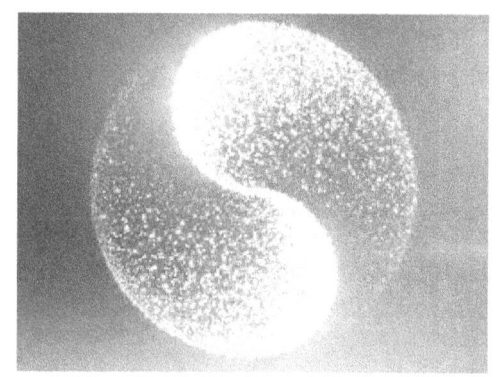

Life is about juggling all of your responsibilities with joy and relaxation. If you focus too much on one aspect of your life, others will suffer. For example, if you are very focused on your career, your relationships will likely suffer, simply for lack of time.

A great practice to start doing every day is taking stock of the important parts of your life. Make a list of four or five major important areas of your life. For example, these could be your family, friends, career, and money (a form of security). Each and every day, take stock of what you have focused on most. Likely, this means that another one of your important categories has been generally neglected.

Make adjustments to bring some balance to that system. If you were forced to work all day, make sure to spend some time with the kids and connect with them when you get home.

The course of your energy depends on where you put your focus. Energy flows where the mind goes. If you focus your attention on one thing, and one thing only, a great deal of energy will flow there to support it. This also means that energy is being taken away from something else, as a law of physics. It is human nature to become transfixed with things, and it is difficult to maintain good balance. Make a conscious effort to pull your mind back into balance for the sake of your overall well-being.

The quality of the energy around you will also have a major impact on your well being and emotional health. If you are surrounded by positive influences and people with your best interests in mind, it will be very easy to be emotionally well, as you are accepting positive energy from your environment.

More likely than not, you are exposed to negative energy throughout the day. It could be related to a strained relationship, a difficult job, or just general bad vibes wherever you go. In your time on this planet, you may have noticed that a select few people always seem to be afflicted with problems and unfortunate circumstances. For example, their car always seems to be broken, they carry on dramatic relationships, and things never seem to work out in their favor.

There is a reason for that. Some people attract only negative energy because they exude negative energy. You get back what you put out there, the well-known rule of karma. Being callous, uncaring and down on yourself only brings about the same old thing. While it is impossible to avoid negativity completely, it is certainly possible to change your circumstances by altering what type of energy you put out there.

The point is, the unfortunate events happening in your life are not the universe 'punishing you,' it is you punishing yourself with your own internal negativity. Changing your thoughts and actions to be more positive can cause a dramatic shift in the course of your life. You have the power to consciously change how you feel about certain events, and how you react to negativity. Doing so blocks that negativity from entering your space. Positivity always wins over negativity.

Remember too that we are mobile creatures, not trees that are destined to grow in the same spot forever. If you do not like the energy around you and the circumstances you are planted in, simply move yourself out of it. This may mean ending volatile relationships, changing jobs, or even uprooting your life completely. It is your right and responsibility to take yourself out of the negativity. Failing to do so will continue to cause negative events in your life. Do you want to be responsible for your own demise?

CHAPTER 8:
Creating Positive Thoughts

Energy can neither be created nor destroyed. That is a basic law of physics. We can, however, change the type of energy coming our way. We can take negative energy and turn it positive with the power of thought.

Take the example we ended with in the last chapter. If you relate to the person who always seems to be in trouble, with luck nowhere in sight, it is likely related to how you process positive and negative energy. It is possible to live in a place surrounded by negative energy and still have a great life. Other times, it is best to remove yourself from it altogether.

Let's start with the first idea of changing your circumstances simply with thought. Imagine that you are living in an apartment complex on the bad side of town. The building is full of people that regularly use drugs, don't have jobs and result in violence to express their feelings. In psychology, we often recognize that raising a child into an adult in this environment often means that the child will resort to a similar life of crime and drugs. It is what they know. What about the select few that rise above these challenges and live lives that are productive, drug-free and peaceful? What is different about them that allows this to happen.

This anomaly shows that the internal energy of a person, created solely by their desires, is stronger than the environment. We do not need to succumb to negativity, we can change it. We are not destined to live less than  ideal lives if we are born into it, we have the power internally to pull ourselves out of it.

The first step in accomplishing this is creating positive thoughts. Thinking positive has the power to take the negative energy from the environment and turn it around. You have the choice to react negatively to a negative situation, or you can turn it around and find the good in it. It takes a great deal of consciousness, self-discipline, and drive to do so, but these are things all humans are capable of.

You can easily instill more positivity into your day by rearranging your thoughts. To get started, set aside a small chunk of time every day to assess your thoughts. It only takes about ten or fifteen minutes to create more awareness in your thinking. Simply sit quietly and think about the content of your day. Think about the exchange you had with the store clerk after waiting in line for what seemed like forever. Were you cordial, or did you let your aggravation show? How did the clerk respond to your actions?

Think about your daily exchanges, and come up with constructive solutions to consciously change your future actions. For example, if you were gruff and a bit rude to the store clerk, what can you do better next time? This is a stepwise process. First, you can change your outward reaction to the stressor. Say, keep your aggravation to yourself and choose to be courteous, despite the annoyance. Quickly, you will begin to realize that you get more positivity back when you put positivity out. You may even turn the clerk's attitude more positive as well.

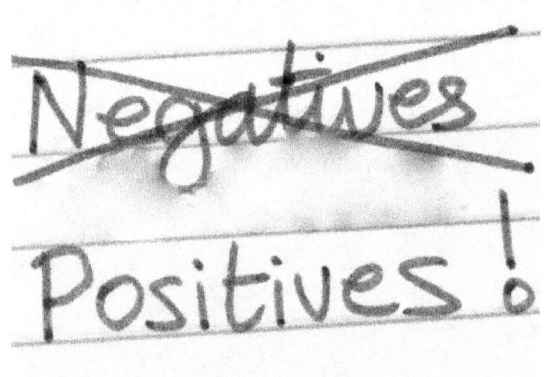

Over time, you will find that it really only hurts you to have negative thoughts. You will start to understand that the small things in life that aggravate you and cause negative thoughts aren't worth the time. So what if the line is long at the grocery store? What harm is it really doing in the grand scheme of things? With these mini-epiphanies, you can then transform your total way of thinking.

In addition to taking time for thought assessment, be more conscious in your daily thinking. Be present in each moment and be conscious of the thoughts that begin to develop. When you recognize yourself being negative about something, try to stop that thought in its tracks. Redirect yourself and challenge yourself to find something positive about it. For example, while you are waiting in a long line, you have a chance to relax for a few minutes. You may also take that time to engage in conversation with the person in front of you. These are all good things.

The brain is a funny organ, in that it is really a creature of habit. Our brain makes associations as a way to process information that is coming in. We learn how to act in different situations, and when we learn what brings good outcomes, we repeatedly do it. Unfortunately, we often think negative thoughts about certain things as a way to deter yourself from acting in a certain way. For example, if you didn't like the taste of brussels sprouts the first time, your brain will elicit a negative reaction to the sight of them to deter you from eating them.

The good news is, it is possible to redirect these associations and change them. Using conscious positive thought on a regular basis actually change the way your brain works. Brain scans over time actually show that creating positive associations instead of negative ones creates more gray matter, and forces you to use more of your brain power. These are all great things. Hooray for positivity!

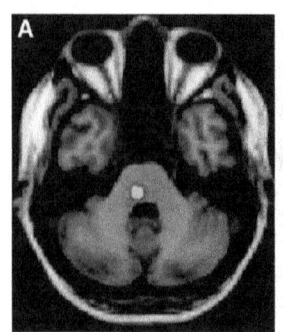 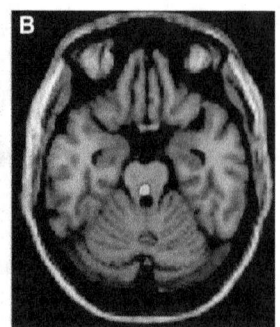

Being more present in your thought strengthens your brain as well as your spiritual connection.

Understanding what makes you happy, angry and overwhelmed is a key to understanding what makes your inner self tick. Your resolve becomes greater, and you become a stronger person overall as you become more in touch with yourself.

It is, however, possible to be weak in this department. Until you are a fully-functioning, energetically aligned human being, it may be necessary to physically change your circumstances to help the process around. If the negativity around you is greatly affecting your ability to be positive, it may be time to make a change. The body and mind are only resilient to a point. If you are doing your best, but are constantly bombarded with negativity, it can be very draining, to the point of no return.

For example, look at a negative relationship. We often see others in mentally and physically abusive relationships. We judge them, whether we mean to or not. How can they continue to let themselves be abused in that way? The reason is, this is likely not how the relationship started. Over time, the emotional investment in the relationship makes a person overlook the negative jabs and perceived 'mistakes' of the abusive person.

The continued negativity draws energy away from the abused until they have nothing left. Their self-esteem disappears, and any shred of positivity within them has been used up. There is nothing left but consuming negativity, something they cannot lift themselves out of without help. The general recommendation for people in this situation is to remove themselves from it, and that is exactly what you can do in any type of overwhelmingly negative situation.

Imagine that this negative situation was actually a physical sickness. You have struggled with a stubborn cold for weeks, with a nagging cough and general fatigue. Over time, you get worse and worse, more fatigued and sick. You would not simply live like this, would you? You would likely get help fighting the illness with medicine. Think of positivity as medicine for your negative situation.

Changing your internal view of yourself, your surroundings and your situation is the first step to gaining enough self-esteem to rise above the situation. This may mean a complete upheaval of your current life, or it may mean looking for a new job. Either way, you are making positive strides toward the life you have always dreamed of living.

CHAPTER 9:
Listening to Your Inner Self

While it is vital to unlock the potential of your pineal gland through decalcification, it is even more so to know how to listen to your inner self. It is always talking, and there is a major difference between simply listening and letting the third eye guide your life.

First off, how can we recognize when our inner self is talking? How do we know we should listen? Let's begin with a short story scenario, one that most people can likely relate to.

Imagine that you are in charge of hiring a person for a position within your company. You get a number of applications and resumes, and you widdle them down to just a few viable candidates. Most of them have quite a bit of experience, each having their own set of strengths and weaknesses. On paper, they all seem equally qualified.

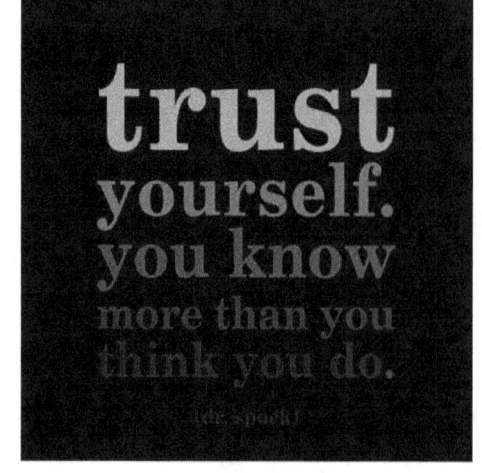

Next comes the in-person interview. You call these people and set up interviews. The first candidate has all of the right experience, great references and a very promising career in front of him. You interview the second person, and they are equally qualified, but something strikes you about this second person.

Although you can't put your finger on it, there is just something unsettling about this second candidate. Maybe it is the way he carried himself or how he shook your hand, small things that couldn't possibly break the deal.

The first candidate, your obvious choice ends up finding another job, and respectfully declines your offer. After reviewing the qualifications of the second candidate with your peers, you decide, although secretly hesitantly, to hire the second candidate.

Unfortunately, after some time working with your team, you find that this person's mannerisms, habits, and ethics do not jive with the company. He is often late, unproductive and sometimes even rude to his peers.

Had you followed your instincts, you may have decided not to follow this lead and hire this person. The problem is, we often try to find analytical reasons to do, or not do something. We can't simply follow our heart, that is not considered very professional.

Our intuition, or our inner self, is always giving us clues, we need to learn to listen. You may recognize your inner self as that gut feeling you get when something just doesn't feel right. This isn't an easily explained feeling, and so it ends up getting overlooked. We like to have good evidence for something before moving forward.

In addition, we often let the thoughts and opinions of others influence our decision, drawing us further from our instincts. In this example, the consensus of the group was to hire the person, and this ended up being the deciding factor. Humans like to go with the flow and avoid confrontation and going against the grain, despite our instincts.

Give your inner self the credit it is due and start trusting it more. In the beginning, you may misread some situations, but it takes a bit of practice to get things right. Try these tips to start tapping into your inner wisdom:

Stop and listen: avoid making quick decisions without consulting your inner self. If you hesitate just a little before choosing to really sit with an idea, you may avoid some headaches. For example, if you had imagined what it might be like to deal with this employee on a daily basis, you may have felt exhausted and a little disgusted, which would certainly change your decision.

Push logic aside: Instead of letting your brain make all of the decisions, put your intuition first in line. Yes, you should make analytical choices, but if your brain and instincts disagree, go with your gut feeling. To be clear, there are no absolutes, so if your brain is telling you not to jump in a freezing river, but your instincts are, maybe go with your brain!

Sharpen your instincts: Getting to know yourself and how your inner self has guided you in the past is a process. History tends to repeat itself, so think about similar scenarios before making decisions. For example, following your brain in this instance led to you hiring a less than a desirable employee. Give your instinct a try next time to see if you get a better result.

Don't be afraid to be wrong: In retrospect, you may find that following your instincts have led you down some interesting paths. Had your brain been in charge, you may have chosen higher ground instead of trudging through the muck. In following your instinct, you may misread some situations, but in retrospect, should find that your intuition is still almost always right.

Don't be afraid to take the chance and admit when things didn't go so well when you fail. This is part of the learning process. We cannot grow and change without taking this chance,  and failure is absolutely part of that process. Think about your current situation as it relates to your career, relationships and other important things in your life. Has ignoring your intuition gotten you where you want to be? Could becoming better at following this instinct bring about the life you want to lead?

Listen in all moments: Just like we discussed with positive thinking, it is necessary to stop and really assess how you are feeling. We can get so caught up in the busyness of the day and let our mind take over, leaving our feelings pushed aside. How do you feel when you wake up? Do you feel relatively okay going to work? Do you dread it? Are you excruciatingly bored with your work, or is it enjoyable? Are you really happy with your relationships or is it comfortable?

This process is uncomfortable. It is often hard to come to terms with these feelings because it leads to the conclusion that we need to make some changes. Remember that recognizing negative feelings and intuition does not mean that you need to make changes right away. Recognition is step one, and the rest will follow when you are ready. Likely, if you have a realization about something, it won't be long until you feel ready to make a shift. Just feel the feelings and see where that gets you.

CHAPTER 10:
Shape Your Life with Third Eye Guidance

It is entirely possible to reshape the entirety of your life with guidance from your inner self. Now that your third eye has been awakened, use the information it is giving you to make informed decisions about your future.

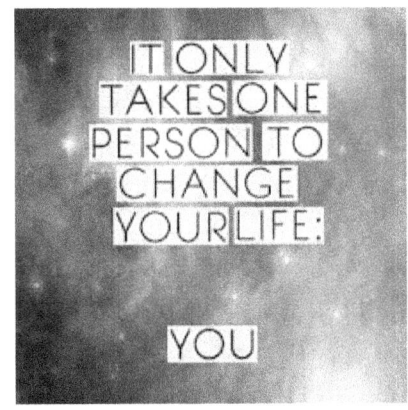

No matter how much time you have put behind you, it is possible to make the future, starting with this very moment, a completely different and wondrous life. If you could have the courage to start the life you have always imagined leading, why wouldn't you? If you knew that leading yourself down a new path would eventually lead to feelings of happiness, security, and love, wouldn't you start today?

The great news, it is all possible, and the wisdom carried by your inner self is all you need to achieve your dreams. So what are they?

The process starts with a bit of vivid imagery. It is necessary to have a clear picture of what it is you want in your head to make a great game plan. Think about making a business plan for your life. First, you must define your goals, then figure out a plan to get there.

If you are like most people, your daydreams of your fabulous life are often cut short by the draws of your current reality. Now is the time to give those daydreams the attention they deserve. Explore what they look like. Are there physical things there? A house? A car? What do these tangible things signify? Security? A happy home for your family?

Next, focus on these feelings and compare them to where you are now. Although your current reality might not look exactly like the one in your mind, it is possible that you already have everything you need to be happy and secure right in front of you. Before you begin on a new path, make sure the one you are on isn't something you will be missing.

If you are feeling uninspired about your true inner goals, don't worry. This probably means that you have been too bogged down with life to really consider this question. Knowing what you want takes time and experience. This step may take a while, even a number of years, to know what you really want.

In the meantime, let your inner intuition guide you. Begin to tune into your intuitive thoughts and play with them. If your inner self is drawn to attend a certain seminar, go ahead and sign up. If it is prompting to move your body and try a new exercise, go with that too. By giving in to your desires, you attract joy and positivity to your life. Every time you loosen the reigns, your spirit is allowed to grow and flourish. Sooner than later, it will reveal your true inner purpose, but only when you are ready.

One of the most interesting places to use your intuition is with starting a business. Sure, you may have an idea of what your business plan  looks like. It takes quite a bit of networking to get any business off the ground. You will be meeting new people, all with spirits as driven and joyous as yours. Let your intuition draw you to positive people and ideas that will help your business flourish.

With any business venture or otherwise, it is important to keep an open mind, and allow your third eye to really see the goodness in front of it. Staying optimistic allows you to explore ideas for new facets of life you formerly knew nothing about. You just never know when a great idea that changes the face of your business may come about.

Here is a little more concrete advice. Each day, take stock of your goals. Do you want to go back to school? Start an exercise routine? Eat healthy? No matter the goal, set your inner self loose with the plans. If exercise is on tap, dig deep and ask your spirit and your body how it would like to move. Does running speak to you? Maybe dance? Is there a class downtown you have always wanted to try, but were to shy to sign up?

Making a concrete plan to accomplish your goals is a great and necessary step to success. Sometimes you need to push yourself through the things you don't truly enjoy doing for the sake of progress. However, if you begin to feel like you are pushing every day, forcing it, you may not be on the right path. Take a step back and listen to your intuition.

Everyone needs a break now and then, so take a couple days to think, relax, and renew your interest in the project. Schedule in time to be more creative and follow the lead of your intuition. For example, if you own an art studio and you have been dealing with the financial aspects of the company a lot lately, take a break and teach a creative painting class to renew and feed your spirit. Making time for what you want to do reminds you why you are doing it in the first place. When it is no longer fun, the ambition is lost.

Your intuitions are the only thing in this world that have your best interests in mind. After all, it is the true you inside telling you where it wants to go. Trust that it is taking you in the right direction, and use it to your advantage. Your inner self is after joy and will do anything to get it. Redefine your definition of success to include overall happiness and joy, and you will never be steered in the wrong direction.

CHAPTER 11:
Meditation

This chapter is purposely left to the near end of this book for a reason. You may have noticed that each chapter hinted at the practice of meditation as a key to all of these concepts. Tapping into your inner spirit and potential is all about listening, and meditation is beneficial to that process.

Meditation is an ageless practice that has been a part of cultures around the world since the very beginning. In early times, people could not transverse the world, sharing ideas, and yet, cultures around the globe have all developed ways of connecting with their inner spirits through different methods of meditation.

The earliest written record of meditation came from Hinduism in India but quickly spread throughout China and Japan. At the same time, it also developed in North and South America.

While the methods may differ, the goal and result are the same. We connect with our inner spirit with quiet reflection to discover who we are, and for the feeling of relaxation and oneness with the universe. Those are all great reasons to try it.

Through time, various forms of meditation have morphed into religions like Judaism, Islam, and Buddhism, with a bit of mindful reflection present in religion across the board.

There are many different ways to meditate, and it is important to explore your options until you find some that work well for you. Traditional meditation involves finding a quiet space, focusing on your breathing, or an external sound, like gongs or chimes. The goal is to clear your mind of everyday thoughts and explore what comes through in that absence.

Other methods include more vocal chanting and even dancing. These types of meditation leave you in a trance-like state, which also signifies a cleared mind now controlled solely by the inner spirit. People often say that dance, in its purest form, is a way of the spirit expressing itself through the body.

Perhaps one of the easiest types of meditation to begin with is Zazen. As you may have guessed, this is affiliated with Zen Buddhism, one of the more recognizable names in eastern religions. This is a traditional seated version of meditation.

Posture and sitting position are crucial to success. Sit in a comfortable position with a straight back to align the chakras. A great deal of attention is focused on the quality of breath, which in itself can help facilitate the mind-clearing process.

In recent years, a newer trend has come across in meditation. Mindfulness meditation stems from Buddhist culture but is relatively new to practice in  Western society. The idea is to block out any incoming thoughts in exchange for focus on the silence of a quiet brain.

Focusing on breath keeps the mind transfixed on a neutral thought. You are breathing, and there is nothing exciting or aggressive about that. Therefore, the mind can simply relax. During the practice, you must make the conscious effort to maintain this state. By redirecting thoughts that enter your mind during this time, you allow your brain vital time to rest and recover, so that you may begin again renewed and ready to handle those thoughts.

Another line of thinking with meditation is allowing thoughts to enter your mind. This is popular in many circles. The idea is to try and clear your mind as in any other. However, instead of consciously maintaining this state of calm, you allow thoughts to flow in and out naturally. Instead of assigning meaning to them, you simply allow the thoughts to be, without applying any logic or emotion. The thoughts are what they are, like paper airplanes floating in and out of your brain.

Qui Gong is a movement-based type of meditation. It takes the meditative properties of meditation and combines it with fluid movement and structured breathing, much like Tai Chi. This method has been practiced by the Chinese for centuries and is thought to improve stress levels, posture, and respiratory health.

No matter what type of meditation speaks to you, regular practice is the key to its benefits, and there are many. Even a short meditation session can reduce stress almost immediately, refresh and recharge the mind, improves focus and increases happiness at the moment.

Reducing stress lowers blood pressure and heart rate, decreasing the risk for heart disease and circulation issues. Less stress also means less stress hormones, which lead to weight gain and a weakened immune system. Low-level stress can cause health problems across the board, so eliminating it improves overall physical health.

Results with mental health are even more dramatic. Regular meditation improves mood, decreases depression and anxiety. Being in touch with your inner self gives you the mental strength to carry on your day, your life, and finding meaning in it. While science often puts a lot of blame for mental illness on chemical imbalances, it is the disconnection with the spirit that is the bigger problem. If your mind feels no purpose, no connection to the energy of the universe, it is aimless, and that is really in the drivers' seat for depression.

Meditation is best practiced daily for best results. It is better to improve and maintain spiritual health than to simply call on meditation when you are suffering. Yes, it will help you find a bit of peace in your mind during times of turmoil, but it is better to connect and be guided by your spirit than to become so lost that you find yourself in a bad situation to begin with.

CHAPTER 12:
Imagery and Visualization

Guided imagery is a new type of meditation that is beginning to take hold. The word new may not be right, as it has been around for centuries, but in terms of recent rediscovery, it is relatively new information.

Ancient Greeks and Native Americans used guided imagery as a way to foresee and predict their own futures. They used it before battle to envision victory, in healing practices to bring on good health, and for a number of other scenarios. Many ancient cultures believed that God has the ability to speak to humans through visions and imagery. Performing regular guided imagery helped spread the word of God and manifest heaven on earth.

In modern times, we can use guided imagery to manifest our greatest wishes and desires. It can be used to imagine our business success, to solidify the visions in our daydreams and a number of other things.

While those all seem like big ideas, guided imagery can also be used as another method of relaxation. For many people, the guise of putting your own

mind into a state of relaxation with traditional meditation seems far-fetched. There is just too much to think about to simply turn your brain off.

Guided imagery offers something else for the mind to focus on, instead of your breath, or the endless stream of thoughts that enter your mind. Guided imagery uses spoken word to paint a picture in your head. This can be anything from a dew-filled meadow, waves crashing on a beach, or envisioning your success.

The mind can focus on the external prompt but builds a relaxing, uplifting environment within their mind. Think of it as building a vacation home deep within the recesses of your mind for your neurons to relax in. They need a break from the thought, and sometimes it takes someone else's voice to get you there.

The only small issue with guided imagery is that you do need an external prompt. This can be in the form of another person in the room guiding you or a prerecorded tape. If you generally can stay on task and guide your own thought, it is also possible to do it on your own.

Before getting started guiding yourself, try to think of some questions you may prompt yourself with. These should be open-ended questions that will help you delve deeper into your visions. For example, if you imagine yourself on a quiet beach, ask yourself to describe the sand, the sound of the waves, the smell of the salt air.

If self-actualization is what you are after, use a different set of questions. Guided imagery is great for unlocking the potential locked away within your own mind. It can be used for self-discovery in all aspects of life. For example, if you imagine yourself as a successful lawyer, ask questions to help figure out how to get to that end. Are you a successful lawyer because you do whatever is necessary to win a case, or do you only defend innocent people? Do you work on the court system, environmental law? What does your success look like?

If you plan to work with another person, it must be someone you trust and with whom you are comfortable with. This person should be serious about the goal of the session, and not make jokes, which can often happen. Unless you are versed in guiding a meditation session, you may feel a little silly and resort to joking around. Not ideal for meditation.

While it is certainly possible to do this on your own at home, guided imagery and visualization are also used in traditional therapy. Imagine you are sitting on a comfortable couch in your therapists' office. They ask you to close your eyes and envision what your perfect life would look like. This helps further remove your mind from the realities of everyday life for relaxation.

As you briefly tell them what that looks like, they ask you more specific questions, prompting you to look deeper at the details of that vision. They may also ask when this is happening. Is it now? Five years from now? What are some of the concrete steps to getting there?

This type of session is great for career development and business, but the same concept can be used to treat depression and anxiety. In fact, guided imagery has been used to allow patients to face their fears without actually being in any danger.

For example, a patient that is afraid of heights may be asked to imagine themselves at the top of a very tall building. The therapist will help them explore what this feels like, the process of calming their thoughts and bringing rational thought to the situation, all from the comfort of a safe office space.

The idea is to train the brain to use rational thought and understand feelings in a fearful or tense situation so that when it does happen, the person will be better equipped to handle it. This technique can also be used to improve self-esteem, build social skills and treat eating disorders and addiction. This is powerful stuff.

If you are interested in finding a professional that is well-versed in guided imagery, look for one that is nationally accredited by a reputable program. The mind is very delicate, and it is possible to create false memories and make problems worse if thoughts and feelings are not properly handled. Work with someone you trust, and who you feel comfortable succumbing your thoughts to. A truly beneficial process will involve revealing your deepest and darkest thoughts to aid the healing process.

The power of guided imagery is unlimited to your ability to accept it into your meditation practice. It can be used momentarily to get your mind to a good place, or extensively as a form of therapy. It is safe and effective, and can be done every day to help connect with your inner spirit, realize your deepest needs and make improvements in every aspect of your life.

CHAPTER 13:
5-Minute Guided Meditation

This short meditation session is meant to relax you in the nick of time. Use this time to assess your state of mind and bring more positivity and light to your day. It is possible, from this moment forward to think the brightest thoughts and live your best life.

Begin by finding a seated position in a comfortable, quiet place. Close your eyes, and take one deep breath. Breathe in until it is physically no longer possible. Hold it there for a moment, feeling the fullness of your lungs. Imagine that within your lungs at this very moment is all the tension and anxiety you have been harnessing.

Now let it go. The air will quickly exit your lungs with great force. Give each and every last bit an extra push. As you do so, close your eyes and begin breathing normally again.

Feel the rush of energy that this oxygen has given you. Feel it tingle through your fingers and toes, as they have been given new life.

Concentrate on the sound of your breath as you steadily breathe in and out. Your breath is constant, just as your ability to persevere is. There is nothing in this life that can shake you. You are strong, resilient and constant, just like your breath.

Your breath is ever-flowing, so is the energy that flows from the universe into your body. You harness that endless energy and use it to carry out positive thoughts and action. That energy is boundless, and so are your ambitions.

Open your eyes. Let them readjust to the light in the room. Reacclimate yourself with your surroundings. This is the life you have chosen to lead. In a few minutes, you will get up and carry out the actions necessary to build on this life.

You will go forth with a renewed sense of purpose, and full of energy. You can do anything your deepest self may desire, and now you are prepared to do it.

Go ahead with a positive light, gracing each moment with light and purity. Everything you touch will glow.

CHAPTER 14:
30-Minute Guided Meditation

This meditation session uses guided imagery to help relax the mind, open the potential of your inner spirit and bring a sense of calm to your life. Use it anytime you need a pick-me-up, and on a regular basis to maintain good mental and spiritual health. Let's begin.

Find a seated, comfortable position in a quiet room. Settle in, relaxing your hip flexors, back, and shoulders. Roll your shoulders and neck gently back and forth, releasing any tension that may have built up. Close your eyes.

Take a deep breath in and out, pushing your anxieties out with your exhale. Take a few breaths to clear yourself of all of your negativity. It is now gone, and you now have space to accept calm, positive thoughts.

Imagine that you are perched comfortably on a smooth, dark rock by the side of a large pond. The rock is almost soft to the touch, and the curve of the rock gently cradles your bottom and legs. The warmth from the day's sun warms your body as it comes in contact with the rock. Feel the warmth on both hands as you rest them on the rock.

Now, look out onto the pond, clear and deep in the middle. It is so pristine that you can see every rock and branch that specks the floor. You see a few fish here and there, milling around, also soaking in the mid-day sun.

A light breeze touches your skin with the warm air and causes the very surface of the water to gently sparkle. You are the only one sitting by this pond, and there are only the sounds of the water trickling in from the nearby spring, and the birds chirping in the trees around you. Look up to see the tips of branches reaching out from the forest, harnessing the energy of the sun, the life-giving force.

See the light, transparent through the round, oblong leaves. They rustle lightly in the warm breeze. You take a deep breath, soaking in the smell of fresh air, and the earthy aroma of the forest.

Across the pond is a grove of pine trees, whose silhouettes remind you of pipe cleaners, almost fluffy looking. The light shines through the needles, creating a soft glow. You see a single bird, flitting about the branches of one of the trees, likely searching for a mid-afternoon snack. It flaps its wings, effortlessly hopping from branch to branch. The energy in this tiny bird is envious, something you hope for.

Yet, at this moment, you are soaking in all of the energy you could need. The warm sun bombards you with positivity, and the gentle breeze brushes negativity away from your spirit. There is a sense of calm here unlike any other.

At this moment there is peace and quiet, no responsibilities or worries. It energizes you to your very core, creating a sense of urgency to feel this way forever. You imagine your life looking and feeling like this every day. You vow no matter where you are in life, to imagine in your mind that you are here, at this moment, relaxed as can be. You see the green water, feel the warm, smooth rock, feel the sun kiss your face. In every moment going forward, there is only this feeling.

Open your eyes, and carry this image with you. Now is the time to live your best life, go forth with the energy given by the sun. It is eternal and never-ending. Simply harness this image any time you need a little pick-me-up.

Conclusion

Thank you for making it through to the end of Third Eye Awakening Mastery: 7 Techniques to Open the Third Eye Chakra, Activate and Decalcify Your Pineal Gland. Let's hope it was informative and able to provide you with all of the tools you need to achieve your goals of connecting with your intuition and the energy of the universe.

The next step is to take action and begin uncovering the true power of your third eye. Doing so will help guide your life in the direction of your deepest desires and purpose in life. Decision making will become easier as your inner self will give you the guidance necessary to navigate through life.

Finally, if you found this book useful in any way, a review on Amazon is always appreciated!

www.ingramcontent.com/pod-product-compliance
Lightning Source LLC
Chambersburg PA
CBHW071407070526
44578CB00002B/507